The Adventures of Scuba Jack
Copyright 2021 by Beth Costanzo
All rights reserved

Looking at the animals on our planet, it's safe to say that there are some extremely cute animals. Whether they live on land or swim in our waters, these cute animals bring some amazing personality to our world.

One of those animals is the **sea otter**. If you've seen a picture of a sea otter or have seen one in person, I'm sure that you have admired how cute it is. But along with its adorable appearance, the sea otter is an extremely interesting creature. Here are some fascinating facts about sea otters.

Some Fun Facts About Sea Otters

The sea otter is a mammal and member of the weasel family. It is native to the North Pacific Ocean, but it can also be found in other places around the world. For example, you can find sea otters off the coasts of California, Oregon, Washington, and Alaska. You can also find them near countries like Russia and Japan. They like to stay within a mile of the shore, so you may be able to spot them if you're on land or in the water.

As far as size, sea otters are relatively small creatures. Males are about 4.5 feet in length and weigh around 75 pounds. Female sea otters are smaller. They are about 4 feet in length and weigh approximately 50 pounds. Sea otters are known for having lots of hair and very strong hind feet. They use their strong feet to propel themselves through the water.

Sea otters spend much of their time grooming themselves. While it looks like they are scratching themselves, sea otters are actually untangling knots, cleaning their fur, and blowing air into their fur. Besides these regular grooming activities, sea otters eat and forage several times during the day. They also set aside time to rest and take naps.

Like other animals, male and female sea otters come together to have babies. Female sea otters are pregnant for about four months. Baby sea otters (called pups) weigh around 4 pounds when they're born. After about 13 weeks, the pup's baby fur is replaced with adult fur. During that time, the mother is doing everything from licking and fluffing the pup's fur to feeding the pup.

Sea otters like to eat many different types of animals. They are over 100 species that they consider prey. Some of those species include snails, clams, mussels, crabs, and even giant octopuses. And like other animals, sea otters are hunted by others. Their predators include sea lions, bald eagles, and orcas. Their predators also include humans, who have spent centuries hunting sea otters for their fur. Because of this, sea otters are still considered to be an endangered species.

A Cute and Fascinating Creature

As you can see, sea otters are fascinating and cute at the same time. Whether you see one in the wild or at your local aquarium, I hope that you remember these fun facts! By doing this, you'll be able to impress your friends, family, and classmates.

SEA OTTER Activities

Tracing

Trace then rewrite the phrase below.

COUNT AND TRACE THE MISSING NUMBERS

CHOOSE THE RIGHT ANSWER

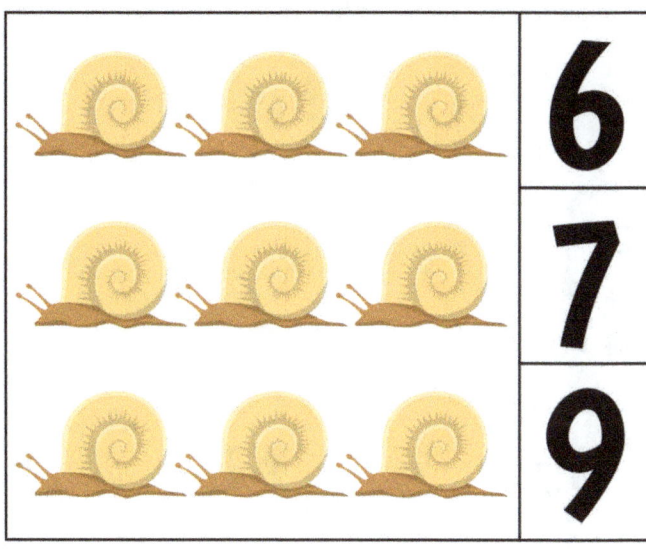
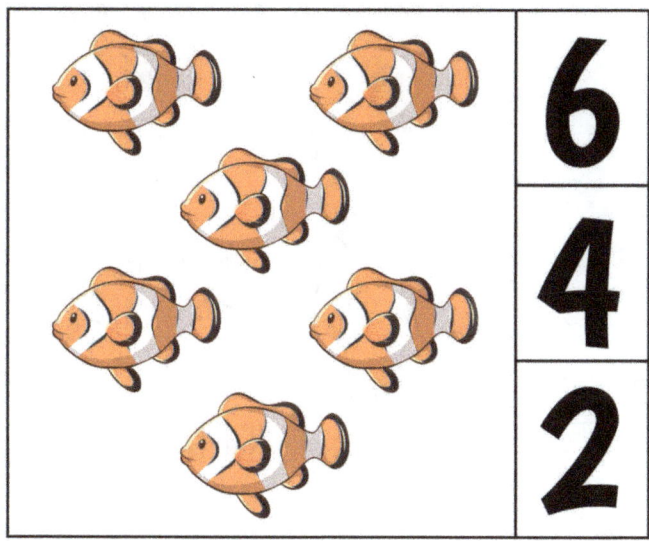

CONNECT THE DOTS

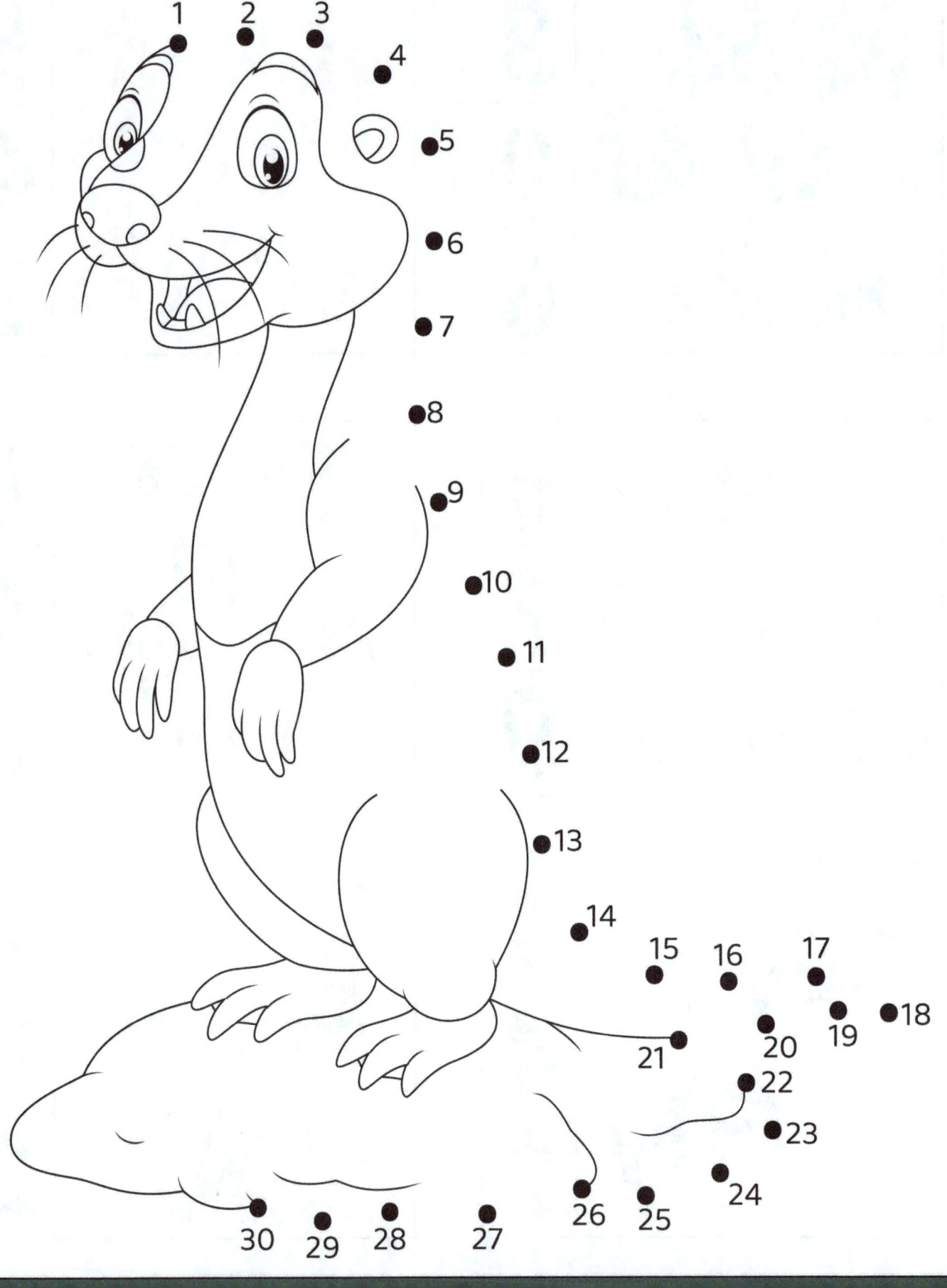

WORD SEARCH

Find and circle the words listed below.

O	H	B	I	R	D	D	U	S	P
T	U	I	O	T	T	E	R	N	R
K	M	D	M	W	C	R	O	A	E
D	A	R	O	Y	U	E	A	I	Y
O	N	M	O	C	F	L	A	L	E
R	R	O	A	R	P	U	P	S	X
C	W	C	B	A	L	A	S	K	A
A	G	N	U	B	M	E	I	L	A
S	V	O	C	T	O	P	U	S	H
Z	E	B	R	A	A	L	M	O	N

Alaska   Otter   Snails   Pups

~~Crab~~   Orcas   Octopus   Human

COLOR IT

SEA OTTER CRAFT

Cut out the sea otter mother and her baby. Paint them and put them together

Visit us at:

www.adventuresofscubajack.com

www.ingramcontent.com/pod-product-compliance
Lightning Source LLC
Chambersburg PA
CBHW060430010526
44118CB00017B/2432